HOW COME AN ORDINARY GUY
LIKE ME BECAME A MISSIONAR

How come an ordinary guy like me became a missionary?

DAVID HUNTLEY

LOXWOOD PRESS

Many of the pictures in this book are taken from very old prints and slides which have been stored in the tropics. Even after software treatment, it has been impossible to restore the original quality.

ISBN 978-1-908113-03

First published 2016

Cover design: Peter Evans

Loxwood Press, 50 Loxwood Avenue, Worthing, West Sussex BN14 7RA

Printed by CZ Design & Print, Bishop's Stortford CM23 3DY

CONTENTS

FOREWORD

TODAY virtually all 'missionaries' are called ***mission partners*** and so I have used this modern term in this book.

I have often been asked, "Why did you become a missionary? What do you actually *do*?"

In these pages I hope, in a light-hearted sort of way, to answer both questions.

Some people feel that for a full-time job in Christian service – a 'vocation' – should come in some supernatural way, in a vision or a dream. Some people do undoubtedly experience such divine guidance, but in my case – I was working for British Railways – it came more by a *concatenation of events* – ordinary events, encounters and experiences that at the time were quite unremarkable and which only in *retrospect* did I see to have been pivotal.

When I am approached by young, and not-so-young, people who are finding their job unsatisfying or lacking a future and they ask what they should do, my usual response is that whatever the current job it is advisable to do one's best within it for a while; and if you do resign, do so in good standing and with some certainty that the move ahead is clearly for the better. Mission service is unlikely to be better as regards salary and conditions of service! It is much more satisfying than that!

David Huntley
2016

1
Just an ordinary guy

I DID not grow up in a church-going family, but did attend various Sunday Schools whcre occasionally we heard about overseas mission partners, usually in Africa or China. Some of these pioneering men and ladies visited our classes when they were on home-breaks in England.

One day our teacher, Miss Cribbs, introduced to the class a friend of hers who had been in Africa on mission partner service, probably as a teacher. She showed us a model of the thatched home where she had lived. This was my introduction to overseas work of that sort.

Brendon House School in Thornton Heath, Croydon. I am the tie-less little fellow in front seated row.The Chinese children in the left of the same row were in the UK with a circus troupe. Miss Jones (centre) was the school owner and principal.

It must have been spring 1939 because we all had to copy down *Today the King and Queen return from Canada.* In three months, late summer, war was declared and the government had already made plans for all remaining children and non-essential adults to be dispersed from large cities to the countryside and coast. However, no serious action over Britain was to occur for almost a year.

I noticed that my mother, not usually much of a radio listener, was anxious to hear every newscast. Hitler was attacking western Europe and France was falling, bringing the swastika to within 21 miles of Britain and separated by just a narrow channel; on a clear day one can discern tall buildings on the opposite side! Over 300,000 troops had been evacuated from Dunkirk, a miraculous deliverance.

The evacuation of children from cities was accelerated and a month ahead of my eighth birthday we children were told at be at our school at 8.30am on 6 June, 1940. Parents had to say their goodbye there and leave and we children were bussed to West Croydon railway station where a special train took us a few miles to Wimbledon, of tennis fame. There, with many other school groups, we were ushered to reserved coaches for a six hour ride to Ilfracombe, a seaside resort in North Devon on the Bristol Channel.

Many other school parties were arriving in North Devon about the same time, some were re-evacuated from the South Coast which now faced the enemy and would later be severely bombed. Others were Jewish children who had been evacuated from Germany and Eastern Europe on the *kindertransports* in the nick of time.

We were 'billeted' with local Ilfracombe families. Because the Croydon schools staff had been evacuated too, our primary education continued on an organised basis. Outside school hours we were free to explore Ilfracombe with its many coves, hills, hilly footpaths and streams.

I learned a useful life skill – how to find my way around and get my bearings in a strange setting!

The greater part of my year in Ilfracombe was spent in the care of Mr and Mrs Eddie Wright. As I was taken to their home, a five-storey town house with a sea view, I saw the sign *Full Gospel Assembly* on the balcony. This seemed to sound something like a church. Eddie Wright was an American Pentecostal pastor who, with his English wife and her mother, acted as foster parents to some dozen or so children. I got along well with Mr and Mrs Wright; we addressed them as 'Uncle' and 'Nanny'. More children arrived, some had been bombed out from London's East End, and many were from very poor homes and had only the clothes they stood in.

The Wrights introduced me to a personal Christian faith, and Mrs Wright often read us stories from the life of Mary Slessor, the Scottish mill girl who became a pioneer missionary in Nigeria, and today there is a major avenue named after her in Calabar City. It was at this time, winter 1940-41, that London and other large cities were being bombed nightly.

By the late summer of 1941 heavy German losses had reduced attacks to occasional 'nuisance raids', and my parents brought me home to South Croydon. I returned to the Howard School and became an occasional attendee at the Sunday School of Emmanuel church, our neighbouring parish. There we continued to hear about mission partners.

2
Post Eleven Plus and National Service

I FAILED the all-important age *eleven plus* examination and also the entrance test to one of the local independent schools, but my parents managed to get me admitted – via an entrance exam – to St Joseph's College, half an hour's bus ride away.

St Joseph's was run by the LaSalle teaching order of 'Brothers', Roman Catholic monks who had been fully teacher-trained in the UK. I remember the Brothers as being godly men who believed in the power of prayer. They got me through the *School Certificate*, and a year or two later I made this up to *Matriculation* – the minimum level for entry to tertiary study; but at that point there was no prospect of going to university. The LaSalle Brothers did not talk about mission partners as such, but told us about remarkable mission-type personalities like Father Damien who served in a leper colony near Hawaii and died from that then incurable disease.

Back in Croydon I had joined a Crusader class[1] and there the mission partner profile was much higher. We prayed for and supported mission partners in China and South Africa, and sent clothes parcels to the latter. When on their home breaks various mission partners would come and speak to the boys and chat with them afterwards, but I had no thought I would ever join them overseas, nor did I have any such desire. I enjoyed the Crusaders' summer camps and house-parties run by the South Africa General Mission and at these I met boys of my own age from other parts of the UK. The aim of the camps was to encourage the boys to understand the

[1]***Crusaders*** was a UK-wide network of Bible classes especially aimed at boys in grammar and independent schools. Crusaders also ran summer camps for boys and similar activities. It has now been renamed ***Urban Saints*** and is co-educational.

Christian faith better and help them to make the faith 'part of themselves'.

At one camp the chaplain was Norman Pateman. He had served in mission in China and held a London first class honours degree in Chinese. He told us about China and showed us its remarkable form of writing. I found him an interesting person. He had a photographic memory and remembered me immediately when we met ten years later!

At Emmanuel church, South Croydon, overseas mission interest was high, about a dozen of their members were serving overseas, and on about eight Sundays a year their societies sent representatives to speak at all three services. Most of their speakers held us 'riveted' to our hard oak un-cushioned pews!

Rather than going on to higher education, I passed quite a simple entrance examination for a job with the recently nationalised British Railways. It seemed to promise an interesting future. After a few weeks in the Clerical Training School at Clapham Junction I was made a junior clerk at our local station, South Croydon, selling tickets to commuters. After a couple of months I was moved to a job in the head office at Waterloo and although this was seen as a 'move up' the pay remained the same; for under-30s remuneration was strictly by age!

National Service

Every 18-year-old male had to register for two years in one of the armed services. With my railway background, I opted for the Royal Engineers which at that time included the travel and transport wings of the British army. It operated railways and ports, plus 'Movement Control' – facilitating the movement of equipment and troops over long and short distances.

First came basic military training in such things as drill,

riflemanship and endless polishing of brass and blanco-ing of webbing equipment. Then followed six rather more interesting weeks in the open air: digging trenches, using explosives, building Bailey Bridges, and even manipulating heavy barges on a nearby lake.

After this 'basic training' I was posted to Longmoor camp in Hampshire for a course leading to a *Clerk, Traffic* qualification. I was singled out as a future instructor and had that plan gone ahead I would soon have worn a corporal's

Bleak Barton Stacey, the cohort for the Far East was known as 'Draft DCCZF' seen here; I am at the back and the tallest.

stripes and been free to go home almost every weekend. But that was not to be. In retrospect I can see why.

I remember the sergeant coming into the lecture room and reading out a list of those to be drafted to the Middle East – a place where it was easy to stop a bullet! To my relief my name was not on the list. He continued, "Those of you not going to the *Middle* East are going to the *Far* East!" My parents were worried because the Korean War was dragging on with very heavy losses; however, to the army *Far East* and *Korea* were different places.

The Far East

It was early 1952. Hot! – And steamy!

Courtesy of Royal Air Force's *Transport Command,* I had landed at Singapore's Changi Airforce Base after the flights from the UK. I say *flights* – in the plural – because the converted bomber in which I had travelled could only fly for about six hours at a time, and then had to be night-stopped for servicing. So the whole journey had taken about a week. I was one of the few 'ordinary' soldiers to fly – most had to spend a sweltering month on a crowded troopship.

This was my introduction to Asia or indeed to anywhere further from Britain than France! I was about 8,000 miles from my home in the London suburb of Croydon.

For a young soldier in 1952 Singapore seemed a 'happy' posting. The shopping offered cameras, watches, fountain-pens and made-to-measure clothing at about half the UK prices. The army camps were much better appointed than those in the UK, with swimming pools, clubs and good recreation facilities. It was always warm, and military discipline more relaxed.

It did not feel like 'war', though Communist bandits across the Causeway in the Malayan states were seriously constricting the population with attacks on civilians and military alike; especially on western expatriates and their Malayan associates. Terrorists had even succeeded in shooting dead the British Governor!

Singapore was still a British Colony, and a variation of that status applied in adjacent Malaya. For practical purposes the two prosperous countries functioned as one. Independence was in the air and 'Malaya' is now part of 'Malaysia' and Singapore is an independent republic.

Three-quarters of Singapore's population were ethnic Chinese and a further ten per cent were ethnic Indians. Many of both of these had been resident there for several generations. The rest were the indigenous Malays. I found all of them to be delightful people among whom to live and work.

In Singapore my job was in the 'Embarkation HQ' inside the dock area. We handled the forces' freight and personnel arriving by ship, mostly from the UK and Australia, and organised their move to the respective camps and depots across Singapore Island. I looked after the discrepancies in the military freight – of which our local contractor seemed to lose a lot. He became very rich!

The Anglican Church was headed by the newly appointed Bishop Henry Baines, who had succeeded Bishop Leonard Wilson, the man who had willingly stayed with his church during the Japanese occupation in 1942-1945, and had been beaten and tortured by the Japanese military police. There were churches in the forces' camps but many were unstaffed; I never recall seeing a chaplain, though I occasionally went to services at the Cathedral or at *Sandes Soldiers' Home*.[1] I also visited the local La Salle School, St Patrick's, then on a seaside site, and the Brothers made me welcome.

On the Queen's birthday, a public holiday, I was assigned to disembark an intelligence officer from the SS *Szechwan*, a small steamer from Hong Kong. I did not know that on the

---

[1]**Sandes Soldiers' Home**, a Christian club and relaxation facilities for the troops, it sought – with some success – to encourage soldiers in their faith. The building and the swimming pool are still used as a Singaporean military officers' club.

steamer was an advance party of the China Inland Mission[1] (CIM). The rising government, now in charge of the whole of China, had pressed the growing Chinese churches to 'cleanse themselves' of all foreigners.

Over 1,000 of the CIM's mission partner personnel were having to leave China for Hong Kong, then possibly for home, for recuperation or retirement. But several hundred volunteered to stay on in Asia and serve by invitation in the local churches across Southeast Asia. They spoke fluent Chinese and had a good understanding of Chinese culture. 'Up country' in Malaya, lay scores of the *New Villages*[2] populated almost entirely by Chinese, and beyond the capability of the growing Malayan churches to reach. Bishop Henry was quick to see that these ex-China personnel could fill this gap in the churches' ministry. I had about six more months to serve in Singapore, after which I returned home on a troopship, the *Empire Trooper.* I thought 'Good bye Singapore, I don't suppose I will ever see you again'. Then a moment later, 'Well, I really might' — and the idea appealed. Perhaps Singapore had become 'part of me', but it would be some years before I would see the island-city again.

Singapore faded out of sight and a month later I was back in cold and overcast England. It was early 1953.

[1]**CIM** – later *Overseas Missionary Fellowship* ***(OMF)***, and currently ***OMF-International***. *See later.*

[2]Due to the Communist bandit activities and insurrection, the many thousands of scattered Chinese rural smallholders were compulsory gathered into fortified *New Villages,* partly for their own security, but also to 'starve' the bandits of food, clothing and other necessities of jungle life.

On a pleasure trip to Kuala Lumpur. We had to travel in uniform and armed, as here with the rifle on my knee on an open-ended coach at Kuala Lumpur station.

3
Back in Britain

I REJOINED Emmanuel Church, South Croydon, and enjoyed its lively young people's programmes. A new curate made the suggestion – unusual for those times – that the *young* people should themselves research an overseas mission activity and learn from it, and also get to understand overseas missions and their objectives. Then the youngsters were to make a presentation to the whole congregation at the forthcoming Missions Weekend. As a research focus he suggested 'Malaya'. We constructed a model of a fortified *Malayan New Village* on an old ping-pong table, with a tape-recorded commentary. I was one of the modelling team, having, passed through such villages myself. This gave us a much closer contact with mission partners then starting to serve in the *New Villages*.

Back in my office in the state-run British Railways at Waterloo Station, the department head made me very welcome, especially as while in the forces I had received several awards in the Railways' *Staff Suggestion Scheme*. I was given a month's run-round of the system on an all-stations free pass, with a view to sitting an exam leading to a 'fast-track' orientation and promotion. Twice I breezed through the examination and the first interview, but was rejected at the final interview! Some people wondered if my later departure from the railway service were due to this 'non-achievement'. That was not the case, though it did make me think! Had I been selected for the 'fast track' scheme, I would certainly have been expected to remain with the railways for many years, if not for life.

I still could not imagine any future outside of the railway and I shared this with a much older man whom I had come to know at a Crusader camp. He advised me to remain in my present employment, *but* if I were to move, *among* the signs *could* be something I read in the Bible such as – and he named a well-known verse. That night, the same verse just *happened* to be in that day's reading. Assuming it to be mere co-incidence I pushed the matter from my mind!

Promotion in the normal railway channel via the grades was extremely slow. I had risen one grade, but many men in their 40's and 50's were still at that level. Railway staff were being encouraged to consider studying, and I studied for the Institute of Transport[1] professional exams, and I remain a retiree member of its successor institute to this day.

Before I left Singapore: I had visited the Traffic Manager of Malayan Railway and he had advised me that the process of *Malayanisation* was well advanced and that any expatriate job on that system, though attractive and well-paid, would probably be short-term. So clearly if I were to see Singapore again it would be unlikely to be on the railway!

As a UK railway employee, I was entitled to extensive free passes and concession tickets overseas, and so resolved to take trains across Europe to Morocco, partly to see the country and also to visit some mission partners known to me, and to see them in action. Their sending mission society *Crosslinks* encouraged me and advised on places to stay.

At that time[2] there were two Christian broadcasting stations in Tangier, both licensed by, and staffed by, Americans. (The USA had been one of the eight countries sharing the territory's rule, and each had the right to license broadcasters.) The idea of a *mission-run* radio station was quite strange to Britons because all British broadcasting was then controlled by the

[1]Now the *Chartered Institute of Logistics and Transport* (CILT) and a much more lively professional institution than its ultra conservative predecessor!

[2]The Tangier multi-national zone had just become part of the Kingdom of Morocco, and the Christian stations had to move away soon afterwards.

BBC and few people listened to anything else. Visits to both of the Tangier radio stations, and chatting with their staff, was an education for me. My trip, as well as being enjoyable, gave me positive impressions of their mission partners' service.

I was invited to two mission 'stations' in the hinterland, where the mission partners were ministering in clinics and also encouraging small church-plants. It was enjoyable meeting so many friendly people, Moroccan, British, Australian and North American, and gaining some insight into their joys and disappointments in mission service. This was my first person-to-person experience of mission partners actually engaging in their work.

The day I returned from Morocco to Croydon I met my (very conservative) vicar, Bertie Rainsbury. Bertie was very keen on missions, but equally dubious about modern devices! I thought he might have seen my trip as an expensive pleasure jaunt, but he was positive and encouraging; he had just returned from the Keswick Convention, where he had met the leader of one of the missionary radio stations and was most impressed with the man and his mission. He warmly commended me for my trip and invited me to join the parish's Missions Committee, chaired by a retired teacher from Nigeria – this, and the planning for the annual mission events, gave me more insights into mission service.

During the next annual Missions Weekend at Emmanuel, Croydon, the senior young people presented *The ministry of Christian radio stations* to an amazed congregation.

Back to the railway at Waterloo, on the promotion front there was good news! I applied for – and got – a summer job in the British & Irish Railways sales shop in New York City. Interviewed in the lordly offices at Marylebone, I was told that the job offered 'good future prospects' beyond the six months.

Before I left for the USA, our curate, John Bickersteth, offered me an invitation to an *Eve of Sailing Guest Night* in London. This informal function was organised by the China Inland Mission (now OMF).

At the Guest Night there were a couple of dozen friendly singles and couples – mostly a little older than myself, but some even a bit younger. They came from North America, UK, and Europe and were to sail for Singapore, *en-route* to various countries of service in East Asia. I found them outgoing and chatty and as younger people in my own age-group, easy to relate to and identify with. They advised me about good churches in New York City, and about visiting the mission's American centre, then in Philadelphia – just 80 minutes by train from New York. Much later I was to meet many of those I first encountered at that London Guest Night.

Viewing the notices at Calvary Church. All morning and evening services were broadcast live to the Greater New York area.

4
A transatlantic future?

POST-WAR austerity still pervaded the UK and travel to the USA was not normally possible for Brits, excepting for diplomats or well-sponsored businessmen. The British government would not release American currency and thus the Americans did not grant visas. In my case the railways sponsored my journey and salary so the visa was granted 'on the nod' while I waited to be finger-printed and sworn that neither I nor any relation had ever had anything to do with Communists!

Life in the ‘Big Apple’ was refreshing; we dealt with real competitive companies and there was no lack of business among Americans who planned visits to Britain. Basic salaries were about triple those in UK, and there was plenty of overtime at an enhanced rate. Moreover ‘merit increases’ in pay were given – something against which the UK trade unions had fought tooth and nail. Oh yes! Unlike Waterloo, in New York there was no room for paper-pushers!

The New York church life was like the city – invigorating; Calvary Church, which I usually attended on Sundays, was packed morning and evening, and both services were broadcast to the city and suburbs.

Another welcome was to a *Christian Men's Breakfast* meeting in a small restaurant. My home-side friends in England were puzzled: “A *meeting?* At *breakfast*? In a *restaurant*?” . . . “What will those Americans get up to next?”

At my first breakfast ‘experience’ I was invited to volunteer to help in Billy Graham's 1957 *Crusade* in Madison Square Garden[1] and also to help with their office work.

[1]Not actually a garden, but a steel-framed, fully airconditioned, indoor arena

Calvary Baptist Church supported some 28 overseas mission partners and several of them were serving in Christian broadcast stations. One or two came along to chat with us during their 'home leave' in the USA.

I was encouraged to consider the call for mission partner service *myself.* Wow! I had no particular inclination to change from the railways, the job was enjoyable, and I had been assured that promotion prospects were excellent. To move to such a totally different sphere would, obviously, require resignation from the railways, plus a full-time study course. This was the first time I had been confronted point blank with the idea of any such a dramatic change in direction.

But I did have time to think. My rail travel concessions enabled me to make several visits to the China Inland Mission's USA headquarters in Philadelphia, and later to join in their week-end gatherings and to hear homecoming mission partner reports. This gave me extensive one-to-one interaction with the young mission partner candidates, mostly around my own age. Should I join them in some way or another? A decision would be needed. But before making any decision I had to understand more about any sphere of work *if* I should make any change.

5
Are mission partners today really necessary?

I HAVE mentioned many times the expression 'mission partners' and so I think I need to answer a few of the questions that are often asked.

There was a World War II poster which confronted you when turning up to buy a travel ticket: *Is your Journey **really** necessary?* The answer depended upon the circumstances and the importance of the journey's objective.

*Are mission partners **really** necessary?* The more you believe in their *importance*, the more *really necessary* mission partnering is. To a humanist only strictly humanitarian activities are valid. To an atheist they are a waste of money and personnel.

But to a Christian they are part and parcel of his belief that such Christian work be undertaken, at least by some.

Christians are guided by their Scripture. Jesus offered his followers, and offers us, a much fuller life in godly love and lifestyle, and importantly in seeing Jesus as God and as a *knowable person*!

He is the emphatic 'caller' and commander to mission partner service. Just before his ascent to Heaven he gave his followers the *mission mandate* to make his gift available across the world.

This mandate, following Jesus' own example, starts with making the faith known, be it in formal or informal ways and, depending upon the situation, *may* include practicalities like medical help and education.

In the realm of humanitarian service, it has been interesting to notice that in many places where missions ministered, the believers and the entire community, *have* risen from grinding poverty in a single generation or two. This effect is remarkable across the broad rice-plains of central Thailand. In the early 1950's there were neither churches nor Christians. Semi-literate rice-farmers scratched a frugal, back-breaking living from their rice paddies. Leprosy, dengue and other diseases abounded. Today, the fruit of missions shows in the tens of thousands of Christian families. All can make a decent living, and disease is minimal or non-existent. All children attend school. Of course government and aid-groups have helped too, but the Christian message is the *great liberator and* ***enabler***; H.M. the King of Thailand, not himself a Christian, has paid tribute to the Christian missions' positive presence among his subjects.

Early mission-partners not only expounded their faith, but undertook much socio-medical work and literacy-training of Christian believers. A taught and informed national church was the objective. After World War II the tendency, as overseas churches came to maturity, has been for western mission partners to become *invited partners* bringing skills which the overseas national churches still want.

This is the picture today. For example, the Anglican Church of Singapore (together with churches of other local denominations) is self-governing, supporting, financing, and propagating. There are no westerners involved in senior posts. Nevertheless they are appealing across the globe for volunteers – western or not – to help them serve in the six other countries of their ecclesiastical area. They welcome full-timers, young volunteers, early retirees, mid-career professionals, and indeed any suitable Christian willing to serve.

Such partners are *welcomed, necessary, non-imperial,* and *asked for*, by whichever church they will partner. Many overseas Christian leaders – notably from India, Philippines,

Korea, Singapore, Malaysia – are *asking for westerners* to partner them in their outreaches across the world. Western missionaries have professional experience or skills which are in short supply in many countries, for example in printing, medicine, broadcasting or biblical/theological training. Their Christian *motivation* is in response to specific instructions from Christ himself and those he taught.

Are mission partners r*esented?/inappropriate today? Just a relic of empire?/Uninvited?*

Certainly not!

Wanted?/Welcomed?

Definitely yes!

What do Mission Partners actually *do?* Then and today

The word *mission*er (or missionary) means *someone who is sent* and is taken from the Latin term. There are *diplomatic* missions, *mission statements* for businesses to aim at, as well as *military* missions and *commercial* missions. However, today the term 'mission partner' refers to those *sent* to help spread the Christian faith and plant churches in places where there are few or none, or to provide further ministry. Even today there are thousands of people-groups who do not know who Jesus Christ is, or even that there is such a person.

Since today 'missionaries' serve by invitation in partnership with local nationals, the term *mission partners* is becoming preferred. As soon as a church is planted and self-sufficient, or some agreed objective is reached, the mission partner moves on.

Many mission partners are medical doctors or surgeons and often they are the first to tackle little understood endemic conditions and to work out a remedy. Several were involved on-the-spot in overcoming the recent Ebola crisis. They improve local life by teaching health issues, as well as by their distinctive Christian presence.

Architects and engineers have often given their services to building projects. Some mission partners pioneer printing and publishing houses. Others serve in the science of linguistics – essential to give a language-group their own alphabet, thus lifting them into literacy so they can appreciate books in their own language, and the Scriptures.

During the 1930's mission-run radio stations first went on-air and they multiplied in the post World War II era. Many countries' telecommunications officials are willing to license these, though most of the former British colonial authorities were not – at least initially![1]

The stations enabled listeners not only to hear the Christian good news, but also to learn about agriculture, health (including sexual health), or to learn English or other languages, or to hear relaxing music – local or western light classical. Many of these transmitting stations could be heard thousands of miles away. Christian transmitters can penetrate the iron and bamboo curtains with ease.

These stations may receive floods of listeners' letters: one of these radio stations in which I have served, receives about 120,000 letters a year from listeners! We offer advice or correspondence courses to enquirers, nowadays using on-line means as well.

Christian broadcasting caught my interest. While still at school I had inherited rather antique radio sets from my grand-parents and learned to repair them and to build simple receivers, as well as a more up-to-date amplifier for our church, thus being introduced to broadcast-related electronics.

The giant mission transmitters still broadcast, but the swing

[1]Nevertheless in most British colonies free airtime was given on government radio stations, usually for a Sunday service and/or a brief daily devotion.

is to using *local* radio outlets as governments increasingly agree to license community radio stations. Christian broadcasters now link their air-time ministry to on-line web channels and most of my own overseas mission partner service has been in connection with broadcasting studios and transmitters, later adapting to video channels. In most locations I also served as an invited spare-part minister (pastor) in a local church. But experienced programme-producers and engineers are still needed.

Who sends out the mission partners?

Traditionally they were funded and commissioned by the main-line denominational churches from their own budgets.[1]

Today the overwhelming majority are funded and sent out by voluntary organisations, many of which are trans-denominational. These raise their money through visiting churches and Christian organisations. Usually the more 'alive' the church is, the better they respond to mission partner needs!

Most mission partners need a support allowance, plus enough to cover, for example, rent, insurance, travel, children's education and superannuation. Currently even a single mission partner serving in an inexpensive country needs an annual support figure of around £20,000! At the overseas end, the tasks are coordinated with local churches, by a Field Leader, who may be either a national or an expatriate.

Some overseas nationals assumed that mission partners were supported and sent out by their home governments. In fact *none* have ever been supported in that way. Exceptionally a few may have received a small contribution towards travel or support, but in respect non-religious services – such as school

[1]Some names and contacts of a selection of mission organisations are listed at the end of this book.

teaching or medical work – which the respective governments would have had to pay for anyway. These were rare in Africa and almost unknown in East Asia.

Do mission partners require any special training?

Yes, they almost always do, though exactly what depends upon the line of service that the candidate is expected to work in.

Typical study could be a course in biblical issues, often leading to at least a diploma, and possibly to a bachelor's degree or higher. On the other hand, some specialists in, say, medicine, may spend less time on specifically biblical studies, but concentrate on missiological issues. Most mission partner sending societies require some kind of short candidature or orientation course in their homeland before they are definitely accepted.

Other shorter, pre-departure courses, may prepare the future mission partners for language-learning by introducing them to the many voice-sounds that come into overseas languages but are not part of spoken English! Those anticipating service in radio, medicine, publishing, etc, do well to gain some experience at home before going overseas.

6
My experience

MY OWN decision was neither quick nor easy and was settled when I was in New York. My parents had grown up through the depression years of the 1920's and early 30's. They had stressed to me the importance of a 'secure job with superannuation', which the railways appeared to offer. On the other hand no mission partner society could offer what the Chinese call an *iron rice-bowl!* The mission society I was interested in was helpful and encouraging, but could not even invite me to do more than 'keep in touch' until I had completed a Bible college course and passed through their candidature process.

The cost of study, fees and merely living would require a lot of money which I did not have. My American friends talked of self-supporting by undertaking part-time work while in an American college, but as a foreign national I would only have been allowed employment in on-campus jobs – like a gardener or lift-attendant. Not exactly well-paid!

While I do not claim to have received any 'visionary' experience – a dream or some remarkable spiritual encounter – I can, however, say that as I wrestled with the support issue in my 7th floor room in New York, I suddenly had complete peace that *if God called me to make a change, I need not fear about money.*

There was one remarkable encounter: young people facing a decision were often advised to 'fast' from food (liquids excepted) for, say, 24 hours to enable serious thinking and probably prayer. I took up this challenge and did not have to wait long, not even 24 hours!

It was Sunday morning in New York City, and I went to my usual breakfast eatery for a cup of coffee. I felt a hand on my shoulder; it was Mr Griffin, the leader of the China Inland Mission (now OMF) in North America. With him was the worldwide General Director of the society, Mr Sanders, and they invited me to join them at table. I only had coffee, which they remarked upon, but fasting (we were told) was to be in secret so I could not explain my ultra-light liquid meal!

Chatting with them, I grasped more about service with their organisation. Neither of these gentlemen would normally have had any reason to be in New York City, nor anywhere near it. One had happened to come for the day from two states away, and the other was visiting from New Zealand! Both they and I 'just happened' to be in the same city at the same time – and in the same restaurant at the same meal!

Just another co-incidence?

I had researched study opportunities in the USA, and corresponded with some well-known colleges. I had also written to the only college in Britain about which I knew anything: the London Bible College.[1] At their suggestion I wrote to my home borough of Croydon and much to my surprise they replied that a grant *would* be available for me to train to degree-level in missions and theology; moreover the study grant would suffice for tuition and living. Of all the 'signals' I had received, this was among the strongest!

Meanwhile in America some further friendly guidance was on the way. I had come to know several young Americans roughly my own age. Jim I met while volunteering as a counsellor for the Billy Graham Crusade and Darrell I had met in Philadelphia. One was a candidate and the other accepted for mission partner service in East Asia with the CIM. Both invited me to spend a week or so as a guest in their respective

[1]**Now** London School of Theology at Northwood, a northern suburb of London

homes in the Mid-West, and so once again my free rail travel came in useful. Jim introduced me to his circle and gave us the practical experience of helping to run a Christian children's camp in the nearby mountains, where I met other overseas-minded Christians. Jim's farewell comment as he saw me off on the train to Des Moines, Iowa, to visit Darrell was, "We'll meet again in Asia!" We did.

Darrell's departure to Asia was quite close and I was invited to his valedictory gathering at the local church. For me this was a lesson in how American churches supported their members on mission partner service. They presented Darrell with most of the items on his sailing list!

But there was more to come as Darell saw me off on the Rock Island Rocket to Chicago; another New York friend, Gary, was on the platform to meet me; he was studying at Moody Bible Institute – of which he gave me a tour – enabling me to get some idea of what the necessary tertiary studies would be like. I now had a much better picture of what a change of direction would involve, and boarded the train back to New York City.

I had seen others' decisions. Now could my decision time be near? Back in New York City, I had to tackle my boss!

Jim and me at the bus taking us from St Louis to the children's camp.

7
The decisive step

THE day that I heard positively about the grant from Croydon Town hall for which I had applied was about the last point in time that I could reasonably tender my resignation to the General Traffic Manager of British Railways North America, Mr G.F. Luther. He immediately responded that he had been about to invite me to remain in the USA long-term, in a very attractive job, coupled with a promising future for a young man in my situation.

I thanked him and explained my position and he was remarkably understanding. I assured him that I was *in no way* 'disappointed with' the railway job (indeed I had all along been anxious that if I ever should leave the railway, I should do so *in good standing*). It was quite a wrench to pull out of something that had become part of me – and to some extent still is!

Returning home on the *Queen Mary* I found that a group of the young mission partners I had met in Philadelphia as candidates were on the same ship *en route* to Asia, via the UK!

More friendly 'information' and 'education'!

I visited my offices at Waterloo. They had heard of my resignation and one asked me, "David, what's this you've done to us?" But all were supportive and understanding of my situation.

A week or two later, I started my three years at London Bible College (LBC), then located at 19 Marylebone Road[1] in Central London, just a few minutes' walk from the railway office from where I had been appointed to work in New York.

[1]The building is now a commercial hospital.

Theology-related concepts and ideas were new to me, but the Principal, Revd Dr Ernest Kevan, was a gifted lecturer. Like a good mathematics or engineering tutor, he broke each issue into basic parts, explained each part, and then fitted them together – a real teacher's gift.

With my room-mates Gerald Sanchez (*left*) and Alfred Yeo

For my first year one of my room-mates was Alfred Yeo, now a retired Methodist Minister and travelling preacher, based on his family home in Singapore; plus Gérald, a Frenchman from Algeria, now serving in Réunion. We are all still in touch.

The grant from Croydon Town Hall sufficed for living and study, but during vacations, and apart from visiting my parents 300 miles northwards in Penrith, I needed somewhere to live and study.

Much of this provision came via our former curate, John Bickersteth who had inherited Ashburnham Place, near Battle in Sussex. John and a few volunteers 'camped out' in the house – then rot-ridden and emptied of most of its furnishing and treasure. John offered students the chance to work half-time and study half-time, but with basic lodging and board. During that time he shared with us his vision for the major development of the house and grounds. He was certain that he was where God wanted him to be and that God would supply the needs step by step. For that reason he resolved *not* to engage in any overt fund raising campaign, nor to go into debt.

This policy was very much based on that of the China Inland Mission (now OMF) which he had encountered during his time at Oak Hill Theological College. The ultimate result is visible today to anyone who drops in for afternoon tea or stay at the beautiful Ashburnham Prayer and Conference Centre.

John Bickersteth was a gifted counsellor to people of my age group; he encouraged me in study, and also my interest in the China Inland Mission, which his church (adjacent to the House) started to support.

My travels to Ashburnham, to Croydon, and to my parents up north were taken care of by an offer from my aunt: "Would you like £150 in my will, or prefer a like sum for a scooter now?" I opted for the latter – the vehicle was enormously useful, both in college and over the next three years. Had I opted for the will, £150 would have lost much of its purchasing power by the time she eventually passed away!

Like other students, I was sent on 'missions' to various churches, both in the London area and in Kent, Suffolk and Central France, travelling, of course, on scooter.

The latter involved quite a bit of cross-cultural exposure, as the French and Swiss team members saw many issues in a different light from that of the insular British!

About a third of the 200 students in the London Bible College had sensed a vocation to overseas service. The rest expected to be schoolteachers or ministers of churches in the UK.

In 1960, I graduated with a London University degree, and

With the French Mission Team in the Auvergne.
I am at top right on the hillock top

was accepted by the China Inland Mission (now OMF) for service, probably in Malaya, and possibly in broadcasting.

8
China Inland Mission (CIM)
now OMF International

The CIM was formed by Dr James Hudson Taylor MRCS in 1864, and was committed to pioneer church planting in *inland* China, in areas where, beyond the coastal ports, there were no known Christians or churches nor even missions. Taylor did not wish to compete with the denominational societies for funds, and so did not make financial appeals – except to God in prayer! This is still the policy.

From its founding with a dozen or so workers, the CIM has become a large fellowship – at times reaching about 1,300 mission partners from many sending countries. This is approximately the OMF's numerical strength as I write in 2016.

The work continued until the Mission's enforced withdrawal under political pressure around 1950-51. The new Chinese government never forced mission partners to leave, but they told the Chinese churches willingly or to (mostly) unwillingly, do the job for them! By the early 1960's, the CIM had been renamed *Overseas Missionary Fellowship* or simply '**OMF**'. *Overseas* referred *not* to the western personnel in the Mission who had come from 'over the seas', but to the 'Overseas Chinese' throughout Asia, among whom they were now to be invited to work. The forced departure of the CIM from China was a traumatic experience for many members; to them it seemed that their life-time calling to China had been abruptly cut off. Nevertheless several hundred, rather than going home, went on to serve across Southeast Asia.

(By the way, in 2015 the OMF celebrated 150 years since the first mission partners sailed with Hudson Taylor as the former China Inland Mission.)

By now (1961) both Malaya and Singapore were flourishing commercially, and mission partners were planting churches among them. Most major towns had at least one church, but some of the smaller towns and villages were still totally 'unchurched'. This was the scene at which I was to arrive shortly in mission service.

9
Singapore again!

IT WAS 1961. After nearly a month at Sea the P&O steamer *Canton* drew into the familiar docks at Singapore. Nine years had elapsed since I had left on the *Empire Trooper.*

We new workers, were driven across Singapore to the OMF's Language & Orientation Centre. Passing through the city, I noticed that not a lot had changed during my nine years away; we even passed the harbour-side office where I had worked for the army. We little realised how the next decades were to see enormous redevelopment across the island. The Malayan peninsular had become terrorist-free, although minor sorties of terrorists from Indonesia were occasionally to threaten stability.

The UK-Australasian forces were still there, but were to pull out later[1] when the occasional threats from Indonesia and Vietnam would have subsided.

The peninsular, Malaya, had been independent from Britain for four years; it had become a federal constitutional monarchy. Singapore was already an internally self-governing State. However there was still commonality of currency, postage, immigration and many administrative affairs. All the talk was about Singapore and Malaya, plus the two British territories in North Borneo merging into an independent 'Malaysia' – a federation of the four territories. This came to pass in 1963, although in 1965 Singapore exited to become a separate and independent Republic, and the commonalities of immigration, finance, and infrastructural services were gradually dissolved.

[1]This longish process was paralleled by increasing military strength of *local* forces in both Singapore and in Malay(si)a.

Both the Malayan and Singaporean governments' attitude to missions and mission partners had thus far remained quite benign. For example, until the year previous to my new arrival, many mission partners had been granted immediate permanent residence. Singapore enjoyed complete religious freedom, but in Malaya itself the laws forbidding faith-sharing among Malays, or indeed towards any Muslim, were being tightened and unified (they had varied from being a vague prohibition in some states to being a statutory offence in others). All loopholes were plugged and penalties increased. Five years later, Malaysian visas were rarely granted to mission partners, and annual renewals were increasingly refused.

Now back again to my 1961 arrival in Singapore!

As a new mission partner with OMF, I faced an initial three months of language study and orientation. I started to learn the Hokkien dialect of Chinese.[1] My weekly church assignment during orientation was in Revd Alfred Yeo's English-language congregation, located in the large Telok Ayer Hokkien Chinese Methodist Church. The Singaporean churches did not really 'need' us, but were kind enough to make us welcome, and to help us to meet local Christians and get a bit more acculturated to teach short-term in their Youth Bible Classes and the like.

[1]Hokkien, also known as Min-nan, Amoy, Ban-lam or Xiamen

10
Getting the *feel* of broadcasting
'Up country' to Perak State in Malaya

AFTER the three months of language study and orientation, I boarded the night train to join the OMF's Anglican team in the northern Malayan state of Perak, where I was located in the District Office town of Teluk Anson (Teluk *Intan* today). I continued language study, helped by mixing with local people of my own age group. After a year or so I was told I would be expected to help in a planned radio recording studio in Singapore. As a base for village work and language study, Teluk Anson was excellent, but there was already a sizeable Methodist church with three separate linguistic congregations.

My stay in Malaya was quite short. After the year in Teluk Anson I was sent to the huge radio station in Manila in the Philippines to be orientated to Christian broadcasting.

Mission partners get time off – relaxing at the Telok Anson swimming club!

The station is operated by the Far East Broadcasting Company (FEBC), an American mission, with counterparts in UK, USA, Canada and Australasia, plus self-supporting Recording Studios in most Asian countries. The many transmitters in Manila formed the world's largest non-government radio station; it can cover China, India and all of Southeast Asia. When I arrived, some 16 transmitters were in operation to provide for Manila-local, Philippine-wide and international beams.

There was a great deal to learn at the Manila station. I had to master a lot more about circuitry and how to resolve problems in amplifiers, recorders and transmitters.

Next came an approach to studio design and then to constructing a broadcast programme script, its requirements and limitations. I produced a short drama series *Echoes from Rome* about the early Church under the emperors. Many evenings I was on News Duty, so from the sheets spewed out of a teleprinter I had to draw up a 15-minute world newscast – about 180 lines of normal type – and read it live. As the only non-government newscast in East Asia it gained FEBC a sizable listenership.

Interviewing a broadcaster in the FEBC studio.

From Manila I returned to Singapore to head FEBC's recording studio there, where programming was primarily in Mandarin for China, but with some programmes in English for Southeast Asia, plus a few in Indonesian. The objective was to establish the studio ministry, and then to hand it over to Singaporean financing and leadership – as it continues today. On Sundays I served in the Church of the Good Shepherd, a 'pioneer' English-language church plant in a low-cost, high-rise estate; since then that congregation has produced more than its due share of Singaporean Christian leaders. I took some studies in the local theological college, and Bishop Sansbury ordained me in St Andrew's Cathedral at Trinity (June) 1964. In my case I was ordained not to *do* church work, but *because* I had already been doing it! A week or two later I sailed back to UK for my first one-year furlough. As a single guy, I was given quite a gruelling programme of speaking appointments – averaging one a week, and located from the north of England, across Wales, and around southern England too!

During this first furlough I exchanged tapes with Ruth, another CIM mission partner, whom I had known from Language school. When I returned to Singapore she drove into the Mission Home – having come down from Malaya for a hospital appointment! Like me she had been learning the same Chinese language. She had trained as an art teacher in Victoria, Australia, before studying at Melbourne Bible Institute for service in Malaya. Ruth had initially been assigned to working in a newish church plant at Triang, another *New Village* in a remote small town in the mountainous centre of Malaya. We had corresponded from time to time in a casual sort of way!

Now, like me she was commencing a second term of service and was developing a youth ministry at Segamat, about 90 minutes' drive north from Singapore. She had one or two more medical appointments at Singapore Hospital, when we were able to spend evenings together, and one weekend I went north to Segamat by invitation from the Methodist minister to preach on Sunday. In Singapore they commented that I had some homework there!

One evening we sat in beautiful cliff-top grounds looking across the sea to the hills of Sumatera; we were actually in the garden of a military mosque. And I proposed to her!

The next day my friend from college days, Alfred Yeo, took us to get an engagement photograph and the rings.

We were married at the church of the Good Shepherd, and our first two children, Jillian and Andrew, were born during our time in Singapore. As our second furlough approached, we handed the studio over to an excellent Singaporean, Mr Lauw Kim Guan, who had also chaired our Local Board. As well as planting churches, some mission partners plant studios!

Our engagement day photo

Wedding at the church of the Good Shepherd.

11
Indonesia and the Philippines

Returning from furlough in UK and Australia, we learnt that we had been invited to develop a similar studio in Jakarta. There we had to learn some Indonesian; our language teacher had us declaiming loudly after the style of the former President Sukarno's slogan *Berdiri di-atas kaki sendiri!* (Stand on your own two feet!) I needed to help tutor the local staff who were all keen on their respective jobs. Probably one major contribution was in teaching double-entry book-keeping to a couple of those who handled money! Our recorded programmes were well received by listeners via about eighty local broadcasters' stations across that vast country, and we never had to pay for airtime. In fact, some stations *paid us* for our dramatized programmes!

Then Lynette was born to us!

Ruth now became more of a full-time housewife, until Jillian, then Andrew and – much later – Lynette, became ready for the OMF school for mission partners' children in Cameron Highlands, Malaya.

We had served in Jakarta for about two years, and the Indonesian staff were competent to operate the studio there. We handed over the studio to Sam, an Indonesian engineering lecturer who is still (2016) heading an excellent, expanding ministry in that country. He is now also a professor in a prestigious university.

The Philippines

Hence with the Singapore and Indonesian ventures now in national hands, we were invited across to Manila.

There we would concentrate on training and upgrading of Filipino staff at the giant station, and also make training visits to some of the other islands where FEBC operated local transmitters.

Our Young family at the radio station:
Ruth, Lynette, David, Andrew, Jillian

To get a better understanding of the equipment, I took an electronic technicians course, qualifying with an American correspondence institute. That's when I discovered how those simultaneous quadratic equations – seemingly needless and bafflingly complex at school – actually had a useful purpose! Ruth was busy with our children during school holidays, and contributed to the children's activities on the radio station 'campus'.

Andrew attended Faith Academy, an American-style school with a close connection to FEBC, while Jill flew to Chefoo, Malaya, twice a year. I was full time on taking seminars for the Filipino technicians, and also worked on a new high power transmitter. A side issue was designing an oscilloscope-like gadget to ensure best use was made of the transmission process. I also led some seminars on basic programming. With the seminar and training programmes accomplished, we looked forward to a furlough in Australia and UK.

Iba, Philippines: heavy outdoor work at the site of the new high-power transmitter for East Asia.

Philippines: Tuning the giant transmitter for beaming to China and Eastern Asia

Planning training sessions and broadcast training projects

12
Hong Kong, Seychelles and Thailand

MORE followed: an assignment in Hong Kong to work with the then new medium of video-recording, which was just becoming available. During our time there, Jill and Andrew moved up from Chefoo to secondary school in Hong Kong, and Lynette started in kindergarten and junior school there. Ruth was active in the Sunday School of St Andrew's church, Kowloon. We were all together as a family for most of the time, and Hong Kong offers lots of things for young families to enjoy!

One assignment was to voice the English parts of a 'learn English by radio' course in Chinese for China. Contrary to earlier experience, the political situation was becoming less tense; now sacks of mail from China, from would-be enrollees in the correspondence course, arrived every few days.

My main assignment was, in conjunction with lively local Chinese, to mobilise the (then) new medium of video-recording, principally for Christian teaching.

Towards the the end of our time in Hong Kong I had the opportunity to study-by-extension with Fuller School of Intercultural Studies. The course culminated in a term's residence in California, and an M.Th (Hons) degree in Missiology. Recorded TV was then a very new science and my thesis was entitled *Video and Missions.*

Back via Australia and US-Canada to the UK. In all of these we enjoyed working stopovers and a speaking programme; while in North America, we managed to get in a little sightseeing – such as a family day at Niagara Falls and another at Knotts' Berry Farm.

The children's education did not suffer. Jill and Andrew were both accepted by very desirable schools in our home town, Croydon. Andrew received a free place at Whitgift School under Prime Minister Mrs Thatcher's scheme. Jill's school, a church-related one, required no fees. Lynette enjoyed the nearby excellent primary school.

Seychelles

Seychelles came next, where I was invited to become first the Programme Controller and then Director of the station, run by Far East Broadcasting Company's UK associate: FEBA. Lynette returned to Chefoo Malaysia, while Jill and Andrew were welcomed to the spacious Croydon home of Chris and Margaret Mowll and their four sons – and continued at the same schools.

The Seychelles radio beams covered the Indian sub-continent, the Middle East and East Africa. Our shore-based transmitters fed about a kilometre of wire out across the shallows to a large aerial array out on the coral reef. Ruth's artistic gifts had plenty of outlets in those beautiful, mountainous islands. The Bishop of Seychelles licensed me to officiate and take services in the island's churches, while Ruth continued with ladies' meetings and the youth work in the Cathedral.

In Seychelles 'FEBA Radio' was one of the island republic's largest enterprises and so I was involved in relationships with the government, and with occasional invitations to embassies. Ruth and I, and the children when with us, were able to take a welcome weekly day off to relax in the countryside or on one of the many sandy beaches.

While Jill and Andrew were settled in school in UK, Lynette ('Nette') was finishing her primary education at Chefoo, Malaya, and she had a long twice-yearly journey by air, as an 'unaccompanied minor' between Seychelles and Malaysia.

Then she, too, returned to UK – to Dean Close School, Gloucester. This was a fee-paying school, but remarkably there seemed to always be just enough money for Nette's fees, which alone totalled about twice our combined annual mission allowances! In one way or another it was possible for all of the three children to spend both summer and Christmas vacations with us in Seychelles.

Thailand

Our final assignment was to Thailand 'for a couple of years', but actually it turned out that only after nine years there would we actually retire. I had been invited to assist the Studio

With Richard, visiting from UK. Banpot church, Central Thailand; one of our working partners, which ran its own town-community radio station, seen here with the duty announcer.

Director of Far East Broadcasting Co, Thailand; but he emigrated, and so I filled in as Director.

Ruth was busied with the youth programme at Christ Church Bangkok, where I was a spare-part curate. The 'children', now more or less 'grown up', visited us singly or together, sometimes bringing a college mate or two (or more) along with them. We enjoyed having these delightful young people in our home, although we could offer some of them only a mattress on the floor. They seemed amply pleased with that! Meanwhile in the studio we were able to develop the programmers, admin staff and the programming – especially introducing them to dramatized items.

All teenagers now: Jill, Lynette and Andrew joined Ruth And David for a holiday at the OMF vacation house on the sea coast south of Bangkok.

Before our retirement, all of the children were in universities in the UK, and later graduated with good degrees. Some people commented that it was missionaries' children (MK's) that suffered by reason of their parents' location and activities. Ours all thought that being an MK was great! The overseas English schooling meant that they were almost a year ahead of their homeside age-group. Later each of them spent some time at Oxford or Cambridge universities.

13
Retirement?

WHEN we 'retired' our mission retirement tasks involved two 'new' (to us) countries: Cambodia and Kenya. Each of these 'late postings' required orientation to a different culture and even some very basic language, as we 'partnered' national broadcasters and church personnel.

In the early 2000's, I was invited to come out of retirement to visit Singapore several times, to help with the OMF (and former CIM) archives as I prepared my doctoral thesis. Some of the family joined us for my graduation at Canterbury – concluding with a service in the Cathedral.

In Cambodia we 'filled-in', heading up the Transworld Radio studio in Phnom Penh for a few months. Churches were being planted, raising the membership increase to about 30% *per year* averaged over the previous decade.

At our first and only ministry in Africa, we were both involved for one term in Eldama Ravine College, teaching Bible and theology to youngish Kenyan pastors. It was very different from East Asia, lacking its glitter and up-to-dateness, but the spiritual outlook of the students was excellent.

Happily Singapore and Malaysia have featured in many of the other post retirement visits. Usually we met those whom we had served with in our earlier days when they were high-schoolers – and now are leaders in the churches.

We have enjoyed having so many Asian friends, to stay in our home and showing them some of our beautiful English countryside: their visits have been an opportunity to reciprocate some of the wonderful hospitality Ruth and I have received in Asia.

My (presumably?) last visit to Singapore in late 2014, (archives again!) included a weekend in the new Parish of

Saigon (Ho Chi Minh City). There I fell head first down the hotel front steps, triggering shortness of breath. The next day I returned to Singapore, only to be hospitalized! They referred me on to Royal Brompton Hospital in London where early the next year I had a new heart valve inserted by keyhole, restoring my health and energy! Surprisingly, this particular operation requires no convalescence. I give thanks, too, for medical care and diagnostic skills in Singapore.

David's Doctoral Graduation: with Ruth at Canterbury.

14
Postscript

DO I LOOK back with 'relief' that I pulled out of the railway service in 1957? Not at all! I learned a lot from my time there, and have remained in touch with a few individuals till today. All of them have done well. I often attend the Chartered Institute of Logistics & Transport's interesting lectures. London's retirees enjoy extensive free travel within the vast metropolitan area and so it's easy to get around.

With help from Emmanuel Church and from some relations, plus a mortgage, we were able to buy a home near where Croydon's suburbia gives out to the country-side. Ruth enjoys painting and visiting ancient cities – with which UK is well-endowed. Now we are starting to take the grandchildren on sightseeing and museum trips, and Ruth encourages our grand-daughter, who seems to be a budding artist.

We are still members of Emmanuel Church where I grew up. But we are both active in St Francis Church, on the estate where we live – which church at the point of our arrival was up for closure! Now it seems to have found new life under Peter, a lively 'Minister-in-Charge'. The growing membership comes from around the world. So we are on familiar ground!

Ruth and I have no regrets – none whatsoever, nor have our children – that we took the step of faith and became 'mission partners' in Asia.

St Francis church, South Croydon

15
Useful sources of information

Most mission partner societies today are trans-denominational, and as well as the addresses in UK many of them have supporting branches in North America, Europe, Australasia, Singapore, Brazil, South Africa and elsewhere.
This information has been taken from the organisations' website which you are encouraged to visit. We cannot guarantee that the information given is accurate and still up-to-date.

Some smaller mission-partner organisations arise from time to time to meet a particular need or opportunity, and may send personnel overseas, financed from one or more 'home' churches or fellowships.

Denominational Societies

BMS World Mission *(Baptist.* Formerly Baptist Missionary Society, BMS)
Works with overseas Baptist churches
PO Box 49, 129 Broadway, Didcot, Oxfordshire OX11 8XA, England
Tel: 01235 517 700
Email: (via website)

Church Missionary Society (CMS, *mostly Anglican*)
(includes SAMS – former South American Missionary Society)
CMS, Watlington Road, Oxford OX4 6BZ, England
Tel: +44 (0)1865 787 400
Fax: +44 (0)1865 776375
Email: info@cms-uk.org

Crosslinks (Formerly BCMS, *mostly Anglican*)
Ministries in Africa, East Asia & Eastern Europe and elsewhere
251 Lewisham Way, London, England
Tel: +44 (0)20 8691 6111
Fax: +44 (0)20 8694 8023
Mission Personnel Coordinator
Email: zleung@crosslinks.org

Us, 'We Are Us' (Formerly USPG, *Mainly Anglican*)
One of UK's longest established missions, with an enviable record of planting Anglican churches overseas. No longer involved in church planting, but ready to send volunteers overseas to meet socio-educational, etc, needs
We Are Us, Harling House, 47-51 Great Suffolk Street, London SE1 OBS, England
Tel: +44 (0)20 7921 2200
Email: info@weareus.org.uk

Transdenominational Societies

These societies accept personnel from across the denominational spectrum, but all members remain members of, and loyal to, their homeside church.

AIM International (Formerly Africa Inland Mission)
AIM-Europe, Halifax Place, Nottingham NG1 1QN, England
Tel: 0115 9838 120
Email: admin.eu.aimint.org

CLC International UK
Publication and sale of Christian literature. Bookshops in UK and worldwide.
Unit 5, Glendale Avenue, Sandycroft Industrial Estate, Sandycroft, Deeside CH5 2QP, UK
Tel: 01244 520000
Email: (*via website*) or Personnel enquiries:
personnel@clcbookshops.com

FEBA Radio
Working with radio stations and studios across the Middle East, Africa, Indian subcontinent and Asia.
(Linked with Far East Broadcasting Co. USA. Operating Christian radio stations in Manila, Korea, Saipan, etc., and recording studios in Southeast Asia.)
Sky Waves House, Ivy Arch Road, Worthing, West Sussex BN
Tel: 01903 237 281
Email – *via* website

Interserve (Formerly Bible & Medical Missionary Society)
Serves mainly in the Middle East and Asia. Strong medical emphasis, but also engages in church planting, evangelism and teaching.
5/6 Walker Avenue, Wolverton Mill, Milton Keynes MK12 5TW, England
Tel: 01908 552700
Email: info@interserve.org.uk

Latin Link (Formerly Evangelical Union of South America. *'Eusa' also now incorporates some smaller missions.)*
Church planting and nurturing in Latin America. Theological training.
Latin Link, 87 London Road, Reading RG1 4QA, England
Tel: 0118 957 7116
Email – *via* website

OMF International (Formerly China Inland Mission)
Pioneering church planting and nurture in East Asia, partnering with Asian churches in outreaches in Africa. Theological education and training. Priority is the many areas still totally unchurched.
Station Approach, Borough Green, Sevenoaks, Kent TN15 8BG, England
Tel: 01732 887 299
Fax: 01732 887 224
Email: omf@omf.org.uk

Operation Mobilisation (Op.Mob)
Short and long term service overseas in church planting and teaching. Accepts short and long term professionals, e.g. doctors, surgeons; and also trains young people through mission visits. Operates ships which call at medically and spiritually needy places.
OM-UK National Office, The Quinta, Weston Rhyn, Oswestry SY10 7LT, UK
Tel: 01691 773 388
Email: info.uk@om.org

Pioneers UK
Sends short and long term teams to Asia and Latin America. Ministry through professional and practical service and through sport.
Bawtry Hall, Bawtry, Doncaster DN10 6JH, England
Tel: 01302 710 750
Email: info@pioneers-UK.org

Servants Asia UK
"...We prayerfully work for the transformation of our impoverished neighbourhoods." Serves in poorer locations across Asia. Christian medical and practical personnel. See website.
Castle Avenue, Edinburgh EH2 7JY, UK
Tel:
Email: info@servantsasia.org

SIM International – Serving in Mission (Formerly Sudan Interior Mission, SIM)
Originally service in East and West Africa, but more recently has amalgamated with a number of other missions. From their website: "...workers among more than 70 countries...on every inhabited continent of the world and serve among many diverse peoples."
Wetheringsett Manor, Wetheringsett, Stowmarket, Suffolk IP14 5QX, England
Tel: 01449 766 464
Fax: 01449 767 148
Email: *via* website

Transworld Radio UK

Operates radio station in Caribbean, Mediterranean, South Africa, Pacific and also studios across their service areas. Needs programming personnel and technicians, in audio and radio transmitting, also admin staff.

TWR-UK, PO Box 606, Alttrincham WA14 2YS, England
Tel: 0161 923 0270
Email: web@twr.org.uk

WEC International UK

Church planting and literature ministries overseas.

Bulstrode, Oxford Road, Gerrards Cross, Bucks SL9 8SZ, England
Tel: 01753 884 631
Email: Info@wec-uk.org

WEC Radio Worldwide (part of WEC above)

Practical training in radio programming and operation.

Springhead Park House, Park Lane, Rothwell, Leeds, West Yorkshire LS26 OET, England
Tel: 0113 282 2291 ext 40, or 0113 282 3908
Email: *via* http://www.radioworldwide.org

Wycliffe Bible Translators UK

Working among unreached peoples, learning their language and giving them alphabets, literacy and the Scriptures. Close co-operation with Bible Society.

The Clare Charity Centre, Wycombe Road, Saunderton, High Wycombe HP14 4BF, England
Tel: 0300 303 1111
Email: askus@wycliffe.org.uk

Relief and refugee agencies

A number of these are also serving as Christian *Missions* in addition to their philanthropic service. For details see their web sites.

Some of them are:

Tear Fund – Refugee and Relief. Handling of endemic diseases.
World Vision – similar.
The Leprosy Mission – cure and care of leprosy patients.

Useful Source of Information

Global Connections UK

A co-ordinating body with which almost all UK missions associate. It provides information about societies and promotes mission consciousness among UK churches.

Global Connections UK
Caswell Road, Leamington Spa, Warwickshire CV31 1QD, England
Tel: 01926 487755
Email: info@globalconections.co.uk (or *via* website)